Investigate

# World Cultures

Louise Spilsbury

**www.raintreepublishers.co.uk**
Visit our website to find out more information about Raintree books.

**To order:**

☎ Phone 0845 6044371
🖹 Fax +44 (0) 1865 312263
🖳 Email myorders@raintreepublishers.co.uk

Customers from outside the UK please telephone +44 1865 312262

Raintree is an imprint of Capstone Global Library Limited, a company incorporated in England and Wales having its registered office at 7 Pilgrim Street, London, EC4V 6LB - Registered company number: 6695582

Text © Capstone Global Library Limited 2010
First published in hardback in 2010
Paperback edition first published in 2011

Edited by Siân Smith, Charlotte Guillain, and Vaarunika Dharmapala
Designed by Joanna Hinton-Malivoire
Original illustrations © Capstone Global Library
Picture research by Elizabeth Alexander and Sally Cole
Originated by Modern Age Repro House Ltd
Printed and bound in China by Leo Paper Group

ISBN 978 0 431933 40 5 (hardback)
14 13 12 11 10
10 9 8 7 6 5 4 3 2 1

ISBN 978 0 431933 48 1 (paperback)
15 14 13 12 11
10 9 8 7 6 5 4 3 2 1

**British Library Cataloguing in Publication Data**
Spilsbury, Louise.
World cultures. – (Investigate)
306-dc22
A full catalogue record for this book is available from the British Library.

**Acknowledgements**
We would like to thank the following for permission to reproduce photographs: Alamy pp. **17** (© Chris McLennan), **23, 24 & 30** (© Greenshoots Communications), **27** (© John Bentley); Corbis pp. **5** (© Michele Westmorland), **6** (© Arvind Garg), **7** (© James Marshall), **8** (© Bob Krist), **10** (© Earl & Nazima Kowall), **11** (© Neil Emmerson/Robert Harding World Imagery), **14** (© Martin Harvey), **15** (© Wendy Stone), **18** (© China Newsphoto/Reuters), **19** (© Brijesh Singh/Reuters), **28** (© Pascal Manoukian/Sygma), **30** (© Arvind Garg); Getty Images pp. **4** (Adam Crowley/The Image Bank), **20** (Arif Ali/AFP); iStockphoto pp. **29 & 30** (© Jani Bryson); Photolibrary pp. **12** (Klaus-Peter Wolf/F1 Online), **13** (Atlantide SN.C/Age Fotostock), **16** (Ken Gillham/Robert Harding Travel), **21** (Angelo Cavalli/Age Fotostock), **22** (David Lomax/Robert Harding Travel), **25** (Marco Simoni/ Robert Harding Travel).

Cover photograph of Lakhon and Khon dancers in traditional clothing reproduced with permission of © Steven Vidler/ Eurasia Press.

Every effort has been made to contact copyright holders of material reproduced in this book. Any omissions will be rectified in subsequent printings if notice is given to the publishers.

# Contents

Some words are shown in bold, **like this**. You can find out what they mean by looking in the glossary.

# People and places

All people in the world have the same basic needs. We all need food and water to live. We all need a home. We share these things with family and friends, and other people who care about us.

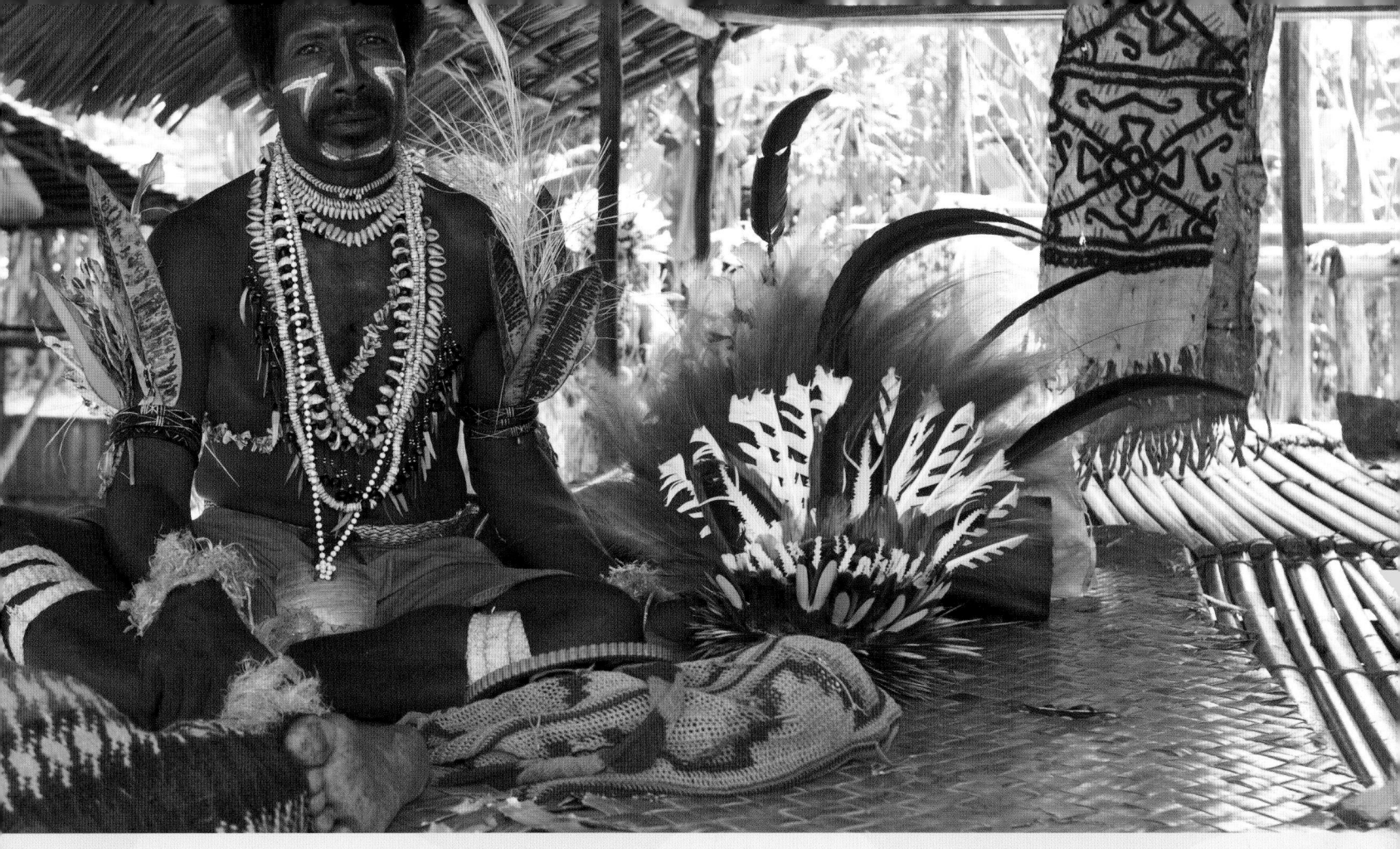

There are also some differences between us. People from different **cultures** may wear different clothes. They may eat different foods and celebrate different festivals. People in different cultures can have different **religions** or **traditions**.

# Foods of the world

Sharing meals is an important part of life for almost every **culture**. People eat different kinds of food because of what grows well in their **climate**. Some cultures eat particular foods because of their **traditions**.

6

 Corn is the **staple** food of most Mexicans. They use it to make thin, flat breads called tortillas.

What kind of food is popular in the Caribbean ?

**?**

**CLUES**

- The Caribbean is made up of a group of **tropical** islands.

- Islands are areas of land surrounded by water.

**A** Fish and other kinds of seafood are popular in the Caribbean. People catch them from the sea around the islands.

People in the Caribbean eat **tropical** fruits and spices too. Tropical areas are hot and damp all year. These are perfect conditions for growing spices and tropical fruits.

People may eat different foods depending on their **religion**. For example, most **Buddhists** do not eat any meat. **Hindus** do not eat any beef.

| Religious group | Pork | Beef | Lamb | Chicken | Fish |
|---|---|---|---|---|---|
| Hindu | ✓ | X | ✓ | ✓ | ✓ |
| Muslim | X | Halal | Halal | Halal | ✓ |
| Sikh | X | X | ✓ | ✓ | ✓ |
| Jewish | X | Kosher | Kosher | Kosher | no shellfish |
| Buddhist | X | X | X | X | X |

⬆ "Halal" and "kosher" mean meat from animals that has been prepared following **Muslim** and **Jewish** laws.

# Games and leisure

People play different sports in different places. For example, people play American football mainly in the United States. Some games are played all over the world. Many people play simple games using stones, string, or sticks.

These children in Nepal are enjoying a game that involves tossing and catching small stones.

**Q** What kind of outdoor activities do you think people enjoy here?

**CLUE**

- The outdoor activities people do depend on their local **climate**.

**A** In cold, snowy places like Switzerland and Canada, people ski or sledge on snow. They also ice-skate on frozen lakes.

Some families do not have money to buy toys. Many children around the world make toys out of whatever they can find. They may turn a scrap of plastic and some string into a kite.

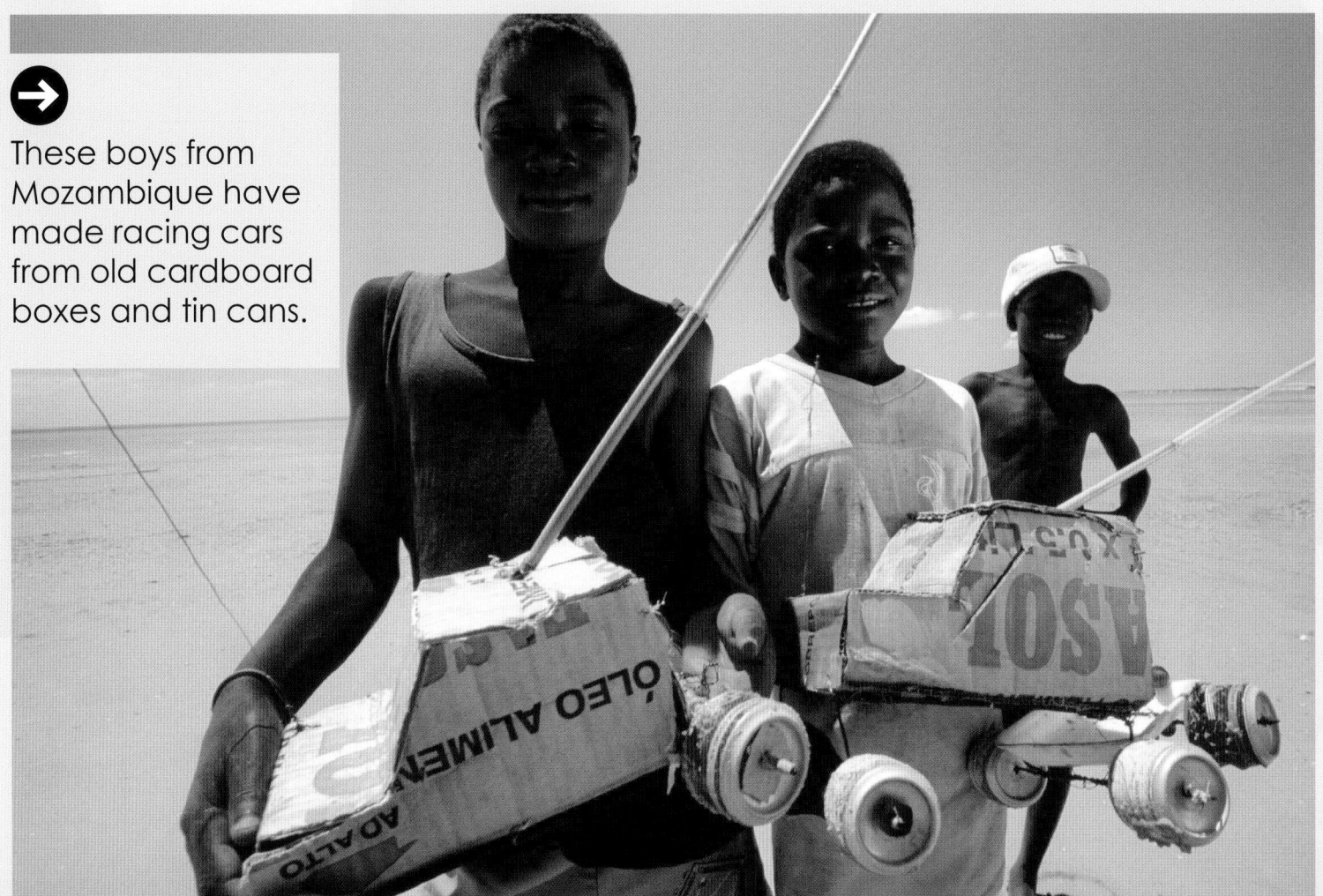

➡️ These boys from Mozambique have made racing cars from old cardboard boxes and tin cans.

# Dressing up

Many people across the world wear similar clothes, such as jeans and T-shirts. Some **cultures** wear different kinds of clothing. These may be suited to their country's **climate** or their **religion**. Some people only wear **traditional** clothes on special occasions.

Where do you think these children in Kenya go to wearing this type of outfit?

**? CLUE**

- The girls only wear this outfit on weekdays.

15

The **Muslim** girls on page 15 wear this uniform when they go to school. Many children across the world wear school uniforms. Uniforms can make people feel part of the school **community**.

↑ On evenings and weekends the girls wear their own clothes.

In Egypt the summer is very hot and the Sun can burn people quickly. Many people there wear long, flowing robes and scarves around their heads. The robes protect their bodies from the Sun. Also, most Egyptians are Muslims who believe in keeping their bodies covered in public.

# Celebrations and religious festivals

**Communities** join together for celebrations all around the world. People sing special songs, eat special foods, and make decorations or give gifts. Some **cultures** celebrate changing seasons or special **religious** festivals.

Many people in the Chinese culture celebrate Chinese New Year with colourful, noisy fireworks.

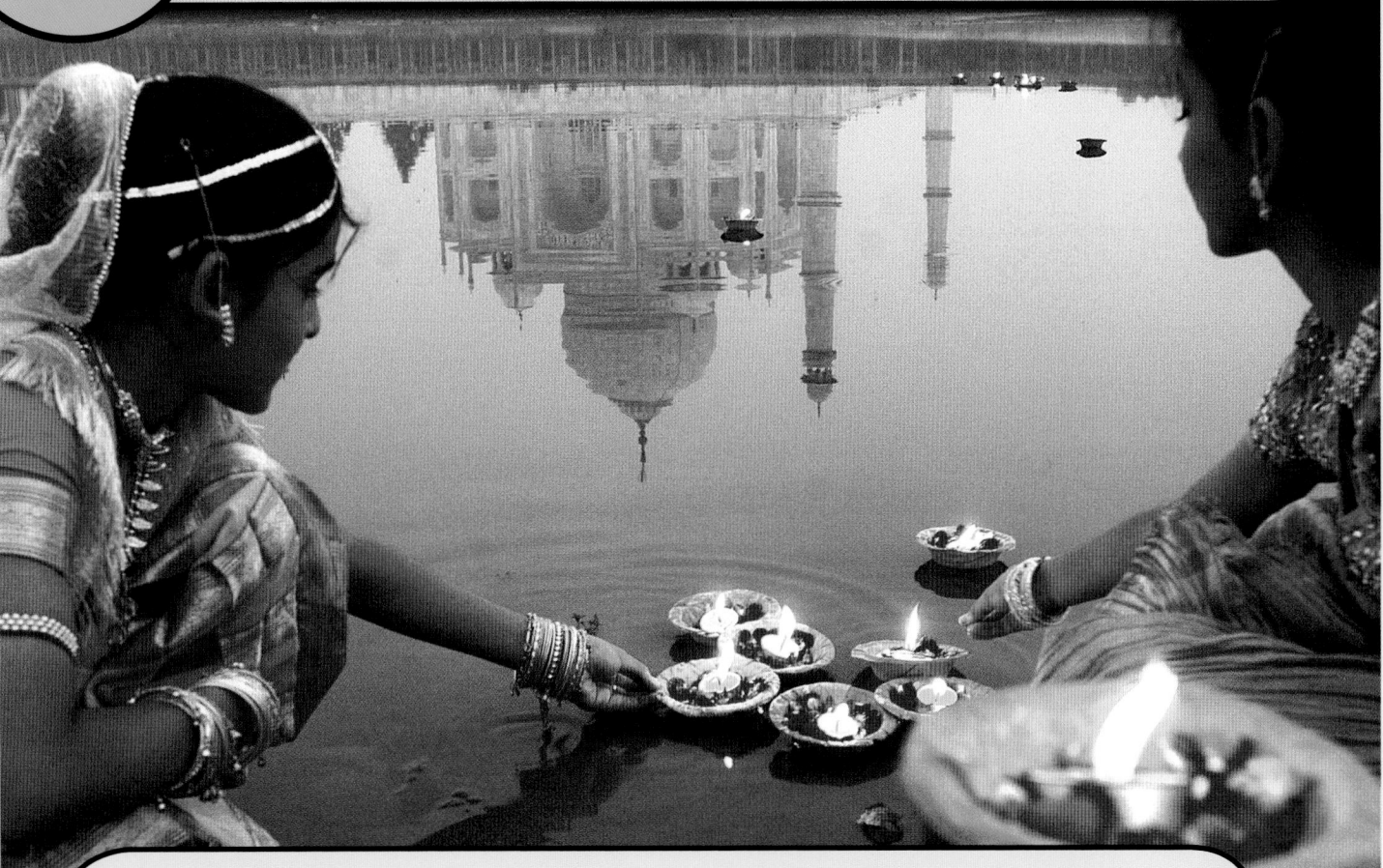

**?** **CLUE**
• What are they floating on the river?

**A** They are celebrating the festival of lights. In Hindi it is called Diwali. Small lamps called **diwas** are placed in rivers, doorways, windows, shops, and streets.

**Hindu tradition** says that diwa lamps help the goddess Lakshmi find people's homes. Some people believe that Lakshmi brings good luck. At Diwali people give gifts, eat special meals, and let off fireworks.

Lent is a time in spring when some **Christians** give up certain foods and spend time praying. A carnival is a last party before Lent begins. In carnivals people dress up in colourful costumes and masks. They play music and parade down the streets dancing.

↑ These people are at a carnival in Rio de Janeiro, Brazil.

# Houses and homes

Homes are where people and families eat, sleep, and share time together. Today many people live in similar types of homes. But some **cultures** have different kinds of homes.

Bedouin people often live in towns during winter. In summer many return to a **traditional** way of life and live in tents.

**Q** What do you think these houses in Ghana are made from?

**CLUE**

? • People here use materials they find on the land to make their homes.

23

**A** The walls of the houses are made from mud and the roofs are made from grass.

→ The homes are built in a circle so the **community** can live and work together.

24

In some places people build houses to keep them warm or cool. In Finland, where it can be very cold, most homes have saunas. People warm up in these special heated rooms. On Greek islands, summers can be very hot. Many houses are white because this colour keeps heat away.

↑ These houses are in the village of Oia, in Greece.

# A global community

We are all part of the global **community**. We have connections with different countries of the world in many ways. For example, we rely on **tropical** countries for fruit like bananas. The farmers who grow the fruit need the money they earn by selling them to us.

Arctic Ocean

Asia – rice

NORTH AMERICA

EUROPE

ASIA

China – wheat

Spain – oranges

Windward Isles – bananas

Atlantic Ocean

Ghana – cocoa

Thailand – pineapples

Pacific Ocean

AFRICA

Brazil – Brazil nuts

Indian Ocean

Pacific Ocean

SOUTH AMERICA

AUSTRALASIA

Southern Ocean

ANTARCTICA

The banana is just one food we eat that comes from around the world. This map shows some of the food provided by different countries.

Reggae music originally came from Jamaica.

We do not just share or exchange food and other products with other places. Much of the music we listen to first began in other places too. What else can you think of that has come from other countries?

27

People in all **cultures** are equal. We all have the same basic **rights**. All children have the right:

 to be free and safe

 to go to school and learn

 to have time and space to play

 to have love and understanding.

It is important to learn about different cultures. It shows us that our lives are different in some ways, but that we have much in common. When we understand how we are similar and why we are different, people can live together and show each other **respect**.

# Checklist

People around the world are different in some ways. This is often because of the **religion**, **traditions**, and **climate** in the places they live.

➡ People wear different clothes.

➡ People eat different foods.

➡ People follow different religions.

➡ People celebrate different festivals.

*But* we are all the same in many important ways. We share the same basic needs. We all need:

food and water to survive

somewhere to live

family and friends.

# Glossary

**Buddhist**  person who follows the teachings of Buddha

**Christian**  person who follows the teachings of Christ

**climate**  the usual pattern of weather in a country over a year

**community**  group of people who live in the same place or have something in common

**culture**  the arts, customs, beliefs, and values that make a community special

**diwa**  small candle or lamp Hindus light for Diwali, the festival of light

**Hindu**  person who follows Hinduism

**Jewish**  person who follows the Jewish religion

**Muslim**  person who follows the religion of Islam

**religion**  people following a religion usually believe in a God or Gods. Different religious groups believe different things and worship in different ways.

**respect**  consider and value a person's feelings and opinions

**rights**  things people are entitled to. We all have a right to be safe and to be treated with respect.

**staple**  basic or essential food

**tradition**  way of behaving that has been part of a culture or community for many years

**tropical**  region of the world that has a hot, rainy climate

# Index